The hardest thing for . ____ _____ __ __ _____ __ give, but how to receive. it is not enough to know how to love; it is only enough when we know how to be loved in return. Charlotte Lankard walks us through that process with tender love and care.

—Doug Manning, Counselor, Lecturer and
Author of Don't Take My Grief Away from Me

Charlotte Lankard speaks from the heart to the heart in a way that only one who has walked with sorrow can speak. Her wit and wisdom will echo in your mind long after you have read her book.

—Molly Levite Griffis, Two Time
Oklahoma Book Award winner

The fragilities of modern life affect us all, and Charlotte Lankard knows it better than most. Readers who share her journey in this heartfelt book will discover their own mileposts in which they can relate, and as importantly, find purpose in even the toughest personal challenges."

—Ed Kelley, Editor, The Oklahoman

It's Called Life is a deceptive book. It is written in so genuine and real a voice that you may be half way through it before you realize that it is one of the wisest books you have read in a very long time. Lankard puts a human face on courage, both her own and yours. Don't even start to read it unless you have the time to finish it. Otherwise it will make you late.

—Rachel Naomi Remen, MD, Author
of Kitchen Table Wisdom, The Little
Book of Kitchen Table Wisdom, and My
Grandfather's Blessings

It's Called Life

To Chelle –

Strength for the Journey!

Charlotte Lankard

It's Called Life

LIVING, LOVING, HURTING, CHANGING

Charlotte Lankard

· Foreword by Jane Jayroe, former Miss America ·

TATE PUBLISHING *& Enterprises*

Published by Tate Publishing & Enterprises, LLC
127 E. Trade Center Terrace | Mustang, Oklahoma 73064 USA
1.888.361.9473 | www.tatepublishing.com

Tate Publishing is committed to excellence in the publishing industry. The company reflects the philosophy established by the founders, based on Psalms 68:11,
"The Lord gave the word and great was the company of those who published it."

Book design copyright © 2007 by Tate Publishing, LLC. All rights reserved.
Cover design by Chris Webb
Interior design by Luke Southern

Published in the United States of America

ISBN: 978–1-60247–452–9
1. Christian Living   2. Practical Life: Self-Help

07.06.05

To Frederick W. Lankard, III
1938–1996
My childhood playmate, my high school
sweetheart, my forever friend.

Acknowledgments

To my family and friends who have walked me through the dark times of change and loss.

To my family in 1979, whose world got turned upside down when I had a climbing accident at the age of forty. I now realize I took for granted that my husband and children would just roll with the punches, and they did.

Our oldest daughter Krista entered college a few weeks after I was released from the hospital, and Providence, Rhode Island, was a long way from Shawnee, Oklahoma. My husband, J.T. Weedman, fifteen-year-old Jayna and thirteen -year-old Bart made the necessary adjustments and took over the shopping and the cooking and the laundry and the carpooling in addition to taking care of me.

To my friends who walked beside me—each bringing their own gift of love. Tom Westbrook, who stood watch over me at the bottom of a canyon. Dot Gorley, who laid her cheek next to mine and wept. Margaret Davis, who walked by my side and gave me shelter. Pam and Matt Goree, who always had time to listen. Max Brattin, who knew how to stay close by without hovering. Judy Mee, who saved the letters I wrote following my husband's diagnosis of cancer. Patsy Hutchens, who made sure I learned to dance.

To Dr. Bill Carpenter, who brought me to Oklahoma City and Baptist Medical Center in 1992 and who introduced me to Kerry Ann Richards, my co-worker and friend—and sometimes my "keeper"—and to Ron Mahn, therapist and friend, who helped me put a home together when I moved to Oklahoma City.

A special thanks to Shawnee's First Baptist Church who surrounded me with their prayers and their love following the accident and to The Seekers Sunday School class at Oklahoma City's Mayflower Congregational Church for encouraging me every step of the way to write this book.

When I needed someone to read the early manuscript, I asked friends Jenny Hendrick, Max Brattin, Betty Craighead, Jan Greene and my son Alan—five people who I knew would give me honest feedback. For the final reading, I asked my friend Patsy Hutchens, who has the skill to gently *tell it like it is*.

After signing a book contract with Tate Publishing, I turned to Steve Lindley, a friend since 1992, who guided me through the writing of the final manuscript. When I was feeling overwhelmed, Steve printed out the list of things to do and wrote "easy" by each one.

My gratitude to *The Oklahoman* for the opportunity to write the weekly column, *Speaking of Life*, and to many of their staff—the real journalists—who encouraged me. It is there I first began to put my life experiences in print.

Writing a column was a new and unexpected opportunity in my sixties and has turned out to be one of the great joys of my life because of the many people I've met across the state of Oklahoma.

Special thanks to Tom Lindley, who was *The Oklahoman*'s editor of the Features section when I first began writing the weekly column. Tom was the first person to read the manuscript and one of my biggest encouragers to write this book.

I also owe a debt of gratitude to the men and women, children and college students, who have been part of my life for only a brief time—befriending me, believing in me and trusting me to hear their stories. They have shown me time and again what courage looks like.

Contents

Foreword

I liked Charlotte Lankard the first time we met. She had a warm and loving offering of herself that was real and without pretense. Plus, I loved her laugh, which she generously shared. It was many months before I heard her story. Knowing what life has brought to Charlotte gives her smile even greater meaning. She's a walking miracle and to see her smile about life the way she does is even more miraculous.

The brokenness that has shattered both her body and her heart would have destroyed some people. Instead, it has made Charlotte stronger, more compassionate and wiser. I'm sure she would have preferred to have encountered fewer hardships in life. Wouldn't we all? But what is truly amazing is how she has allowed God to use her difficulties to help others. It has enabled her to write honestly about her pain and experiences—never playing the victim or the hero.

It has been my privilege to be in several faith development groups with Charlotte, and I'm always amazed by her ability to comfort a hurting heart in another person. She does it with a professional mind and loving spirit. You'll come to understand that special role Charlotte plays for others as you read her story. Her gift for transforming her most personal feelings into powerful words of comfort will be a gift to you, as well.

Charlotte grew up in small town Oklahoma, a preacher's daughter and the only child of adoring parents. Her happy, typical Oklahoma world later expanded to include a husband and children, who were her focus for the first forty years of her life. Then, everything changed. Talk about falling off a cliff!

I can remember when the bottom fell out of my world. I thought the pain would never go away. It was so hard to function. I questioned whether there would ever be a day that the sun would shine on me again. As I worked my way back to the living, there were many elements that helped me find my way. One of them came in the form of books written by people who really understood deep emotional pain. Charlotte has written such a book. I know it will help people from all walks of life and in all forms of darkness.

May we all learn courage and gain hope by sharing Charlotte's story and stepping into a friendship with this remarkable woman.

—Jane Jayroe, former Miss America, television news anchor, Oklahoma Cabinet Secretary of Oklahoma. Co-author of *More Grace than Glamour*.

Introduction

You can't be brave if you've only had wonderful things happen to you.

—Mary Tyler Moore

I don't know of anyone who lives a long time who has not been wounded in some way. It is called life, and it happens to us all.

There are families who go hungry and illnesses that cripple people and diminish their quality of life. Others bury a parent or a child, and some live with pain inside that no one knows or sees.

In my practice as a marriage and family therapist, I have heard many stories of physical and emotional abuse that people received as children. There are adults who hit and bruise and hurt. There are also adults who would never hit a child, but instead frighten and shame and criticize until little self-worth remains, leaving scars inside far worse than ones that are visible.

But there are also the fortunate few whose early lives are safe and protected, who have enough food to eat and clothes to wear and are loved by people they can trust. I was one of those.

I was an only child, born to C. T. and Mary Perkins on February 23, 1939, in Shawnee, Oklahoma. My parents had lost a son at birth ten years before and were told the chances of having another child were slim. Needless to say, I was wanted, welcomed and cherished.

My father was a Southern Baptist preacher, and my mother a full-time homemaker who as far back as I can remember was always the church pianist.

C. T. and Mary Perkins were not perfect parents, and at a younger age I could list off what I didn't like about the way I was raised. My dad was too rigid and restrictive, and my mother was too passive. Now in my late sixties, I can tell you what they did right.

My preacher father, who died at the age of eighty-six, was the maker and keeper of the rules—the guidelines for our behavior. The *dos and don'ts* were clear and not up for discussion.

My favorite memory as a young child with my father is that of being held up against him, my head resting on his shoulder as he would rock me to sleep, patting my back rhythmically as though keeping time to music. And always, I can see him in the pulpit doing what he loved best—preaching.

My mother, 98 years old when she died, was a gentle woman and always kind—not only to me, but to everyone, whether a friend or a stranger.

I do not remember her ever being too busy when I

wanted her attention, and she often said to me, "Charlotte Sue, you are just like your father, you can do anything you set your mind to." (We would now call that building good self-esteem.)

I do not remember her ever yelling or screaming or criticizing. When I made mistakes or behaved in a way that would have not been acceptable to my father, she would talk privately with me about it and the subject was never brought up again. I never knew if she told my father.

When I was three years old, we moved to Crescent, Oklahoma, where my dad served as pastor of the First Baptist Church. During my eleventh year, we moved to Kingfisher, Oklahoma, one block from the junior high/ high school campus and next door to Fred and Dorothy Lankard, their son Freddie and dog Stubby. Freddie was my age, in the same class, and a great help in introducing me to my new classmates.

The move to Kingfisher transitioned my father from being a church pastor to what was then called an Associational Missionary, under the auspices of the Baptist General Convention of Oklahoma. His job was to assist the Baptist churches in three counties in whatever way they needed and to help establish new churches in areas that had none.

Regardless of where I lived I was always "the preacher's kid," and my father constantly reminded me it was my responsibility to be a good example to other people's children. This meant he did not allow me to attend movies or dances, wear shorts or participate in "mixed bathing"— his words for swimming. His restrictions meant I was often left out of school and social activities. No girls' basketball or tennis or swimming—activities that required baring too much skin. No school dances or "Teen Town" dances.

In spite of that, I was blessed with close friends and enjoyed recognition from my teachers and my peers. I was always an active member of the church's youth group and at Kingfisher High School, some of my favorite memories are class officer, student council member, French horn player in the high school marching band, and a delegate to Oklahoma Girls State in 1956.

Those activities and friendships served to balance the many restrictions dictated by my father. But what I now understand is there was a gift that came from living with all those limits. It may have been from those many rules laid down by my father that I first learned to accept things I could not change. That awareness was likely reinforced by the many sermons I heard based on the New Testament book of Philippians 4:12–13:

> I know what it is to be in need, and I know what it is to have plenty. I have learned the secret of being content in any and every situation, whether well fed or hungry, whether living in plenty or in want. I can do everything through Him who gives me strength.

As a result, throughout my life, I have seldom spent time fretting about—or fighting against—what I could not do or could not have. Now I can recognize this as a coping skill that has served me well when facing those experiences which interrupted my life and over which I was helpless to change.

I remember our life as a family as quiet, simple, totally centered around church activities and filled with other loving families who held me and hugged me and took me home with them—to farms and featherbeds, to modest homes filled with laughter and good food, to beautiful homes that taught me about travel and a world outside the one I lived with my parents.

Almost by osmosis, I was provided a strong spiritual foundation. The scriptures I memorized, the sermons I heard, and the opportunity to watch as my parents walked with other families through births and deaths, tragedies and new beginnings, taught me as a child that life brings both good times and difficult times.

I listened as my father reminded congregations that whatever might come, they could depend on a loving Heavenly Father who would always walk beside them— guiding, protecting, sustaining and daily providing them whatever they might need. And so I believed that for myself.

I was not a spoiled child because there were many restrictions and many things I was not allowed growing up, but there is no doubt I was well loved.

My parents could have written the words penned by Maureen Hawkins:

"Before you were conceived I wanted you. Before you were born I loved you. Before you were here an hour I would die for you. This is the miracle of life."

Being loved that much is great pressure for a child who always felt responsible for her parent's happiness, but at the same time, I now understand how fortunate I was to have such a solid foundation upon which to begin the journey of living my life.

After graduation from high school and two years of college, I married at the age of twenty to J. T. Weedman, a young man four years older. J.T. was willing to work hard to provide me, and our three children, with a comfortable home, travel and educational opportunities.

In addition to being a wife and mother, I completed a bachelor's and a master's degree and in my late thirties, I began to work with college students at First Baptist Church in Shawnee, Oklahoma, where my family and I were members. Most of them were students at Oklahoma Baptist University (OBU).

The first thirty-nine years of my life were simple and easy. I was provided for and cared for by my parents and my husband. I never had to worry about material needs. I enjoyed my children and the new work I was beginning with young adults.

It was the beginning of my fortieth year when my easy world turned upside down in a place known as the Forty Foot Hole Canyon.

Life Is a Risky Business

> You gain strength, courage and confidence by every experience in which you really stop to look fear in the face. You must do the thing, which you think you cannot do.
>
> —Eleanor Roosevelt

The Forty Foot Hole Canyon is a wild and beautiful spot with a steep slit in the rocks on the western edge of the Wichita Mountains National Park Wildlife Refuge, northwest of Lawton, Oklahoma, not far from where the real West begins.

It is here a group of us had chosen to spend the day climbing to the top of the steep cliffs and then rappelling down a sheer 125-foot drop to the canyon floor below.

People have often asked me, "Why at the age of forty, would you even want to do something like that?" I can only make some guesses. Part of me thinks if you don't take some risks and put yourself out on a limb for some adventures when you're a teenager, you'll do it later as an adult. And I had not been a risk-taker as a young person.

It may also have to do with the fact that I had always been strong and athletic and enjoyed mental and physical challenges. Plus, this was not my first time to rappel. My first time was four years earlier at Hinton, Oklahoma's Red Rock Canyon and from then on was I was "hooked."

So here I was June 30, 1979, in another beautiful canyon. The temperature that day would hit 110 degrees, even hotter than usual for a place that produces its fair share of summer scorchers. With a group of seventeen OBU students, five other adults and my fifteen-year-old daughter Jayna, we had departed Shawnee before sunrise, cooked breakfast by the side of the road and then entered the Wildlife Refuge and hiked into the canyon.

We spent the day climbing to the top and rappelling down. It was a scorcher but at the end of the canyon was a wonderful forty-foot swimming hole that provided a respite from the heat.

About 3:30 in the afternoon, most of the students were cooling off in the water, and Paul Calmes, Minister of Education for Shawnee's First Baptist Church, and I climbed up the side of the cliff for "one last time down."

I remember leaning over to him as we stepped backwards off the cliff and saying teasingly, "I bet I can beat you to the bottom."

As I pushed off to begin my descent, little did I know that two hours later, I would go out in an Army helicopter, piloted by an Army MediVac team from nearby Ft. Sill Military Reservation, with multiple broken ribs and vertebrae, a pelvic fracture, a crushed left heel, a laceration on the back of my head and still unknown, but probable, internal injuries.

Paul, at the top, and adults and students below, had watched in horror as the rope spun free of the carabiner and I dropped an estimated sixty to eighty feet, in a standing up position, to the canyon floor below. I landed first on my left heel, bounced up in the air about ten feet and came down in a sitting position on my right hip, then flipped over on my back.

The rescue team who later airlifted me out of the canyon told us it looked as though the carabiner was popped open by the rope passing through it and pressing against it. Today we would use D-rings instead—shaped like a "D"—and even that is rarely used for rapid descent. For a rapid descent they use an "eight," a solid figure in the shape of the numeral 8 with no possibility of opening, as opposed to the carabiner that had to be screwed shut.

My recollection of that afternoon is that the adults were quickly to my side, holding my hand, assessing the damage and knowing we needed help. Some of the young men raced out to the main road to find a ranger station. Earlier that morning, we had taken thirty minutes to hike in from the main road. I was later told that David Mair and Craig Koontz ran out in eight.

The other students and my fifteen-year-old daughter Jayna, who had heard me hit, gathered on a ledge a few feet above me and through tears spoke encouraging words to me.

I remember the pain, unlike anything I'd ever known. But I don't remember being afraid. I felt as though it was my job to take care of the young people and assure them I was okay and would be just fine. People explain that by telling me I was in shock. All I know is it helped me maintain my composure under some very frightening conditions.

"Why Charlotte?" I overheard a student say.

"Why not Charlotte?" answered Diane Hays, another student. "Can you think of anyone who could handle it better?"

Through the pain, I remember being struck with two feelings when I heard those words—pride and pressure. Pride that she thought I could handle it, and pressure not to disappoint anyone.

While I was lying at the bottom of the canyon trying not to let anyone know the kind of pain I was in and feeling like I had to be brave for of all of them—above the canyon the race to save my life was on. Due to the spiraling temperature that summer afternoon and the narrow walls of the canyon, it was an hour and half later before help would come.

Years later, Tom Westbrook, my friend and our team leader, tells me there was much going on outside of me that I did not know about that day:

We sent two sets of runners to the cars, a hike of close to one mile over difficult terrain. They were able to call the Comanche County Memorial Hospital who directed them to Fort Sill, and Fort Sill dispatched their first operational team for MATS—Military Air Transport System.

Three of the soldiers were medics and trained in Vietnam. One of the guys was a doctor. As soon as they landed up above, we rappelled the doctor down to you with his kit bags. He stabilized your neck and spine, and we moved you on to a back board (the word torture comes to mind).

I do not think I lost consciousness, but I have only sketchy memories of that long wait. I remember being unable to move and the excruciating pain because of all the broken bones.

I remember hearing thunder and students saying they

were afraid it was going to rain and someone building a makeshift tent to cover me.

I remember the hushed voices and the worried look of the adults directly in front of me, the tears of students looking down at me, and the voice of my fifteen-year-old daughter, through heavy sobs, saying to me over and over, "Oh Mom, if Daddy was here he'd be so proud of you, and I *know* God's proud of you."

While I was working hard not to "let Daddy and God down," Tom was faced with the difficulties of getting me out of the canyon:

We all believed that getting you up the canyon wall to the place where the helicopter dropped off the doctor would be truly difficult, jostling and painful, and consume extreme time to rig up two more ropes. Plus, the chopper had no winch and no basket in which to carry you and lift you out of the canyon.

The pilots then came up with a daring plan. Charlotte, the clearance of that chopper's blades was less than fifteen feet on either side of the canyon wall. The temperature was 110 degrees according to their weather guys on the flight range.

Thunderstorms were closing in—turbulent, and the moisture making for thin air.

One man flew rotor and the other flew tail to put that Huey in the canyon so we would not have to take time to haul you up and then load you in from the top.

We shielded you from the wind and debris, but that noise and wind completely filled every aspect of that canyon.

I remember one of the adults, Jan Tipton, aiming the movie camera at the helicopter as it hovered above and finally came in for the rescue. (Later I learned the soldiers from Ft. Sill asked for a copy of the film. The only problem was Jan had never pushed the "on" button.)

I remember students frantically waving their arms as the helicopter hovered overhead for what felt like a very long time before the soldiers finally entered the canyon, several yards upstream.

Tom recalls further challenges in the rescue:

The chopper never landed because there was no level place in which to set down the skids. It would have tilted and the blades would have made mincemeat of us all. Those pilots held that chopper three feet off of the water. The soldiers, with the help of some of the students, carried you upstream over slippery, moss-covered rocks and handed your stretcher up into the waiting helicopter.

Tom concludes his account, which includes his unexpected way to make sure I made it out of the canyon alive:

Again, remember it was only the second operational week of this MATS team and you were their first truly challenging 'helicopter is the only way' patient. They had you in the emergency room of the Comanche County Memorial Hospital in 1/10 of the time it would have taken to get an ambulance out to the parking lot, get a back board and team down to you, stabilize you, portage you out, put you in an ambulance and drive you into Lawton.

I must tell you my largest fear for you was shock. I knew you would stay warm on the warm rock where your body rested, but you were at an angle, head up and feet down, meaning that the blood from all the broken bones could pool in your lower extremities as your body began to shut down.

You had no external wounds except for a gouge on the ankle and minor cuts with venuous bleeding on your back and leg. There was no bleeding from eyes, ears, nose or mouth. Once we stabilized you as much as possible (on the rock again, with a small blanket under you, did I mention "torture?") *we shaded you from the sun and kept your mouth wet, without giving you fluids.*

What I did not tell anyone else was that every time that I thought I was losing, you, I nudged your ankle with my boot. I knew it was painful for two reasons. One, you had broken bones, and two, you had an open wound with a little rock in there. It was the most terrible thing I have done repeatedly to someone, but three or four times, you would begin to doze and I would nudge that ankle until you 'swam out' of the shock because of the pain. It was my only 'tool,' and I am sorry for that added pain.

As soon as they loaded me into the helicopter, an oxygen mask was placed over my face and ear protectors covered my ears to muffle the noise. For the first time since the fall, and without any distractions, I was alone with pain that washed over me as the helicopter lifted off. I cannot describe it, other than to tell you it was overwhelming and like nothing I had ever experienced. I had never before known helplessness. Now, I was surrounded by it.

The X Factor

Life's under no obligation to give us what we expect.

—Margaret Mitchell

I must have finally lost consciousness during the helicopter ride because my next memory is lying on a stretcher in the emergency room of the Comanche County Memorial Hospital. Excruciating pain woke me as hospital personnel tried to remove my bloody clothing.

With the tiniest movement of my broken body, the pain would wash over me and I quickly gave permission to cut the clothes off.

A few minutes later a nurse approached me with a razor telling me she was going to shave off my hair so they could stitch up a head wound. I remember my absolute horror at the thought of being a bald forty-year-old woman. I may have been bleeding to death, but my female vanity was alive and well, and I insisted they only shave the small area they'd be stitching.

Next came the X-ray tables, cold and hard, and with every movement, a wave of pain that felt close to unbearable. I remember wishing I had developed "the fine art of fainting." That did not happen and I began my long journey with unending and gradually worsening pain that would go on for the next twenty-two years.

Later that evening my husband and son arrived from Shawnee. Tom told me later how hard it was for him to greet J.T.:

The hardest time I ever had to meet a man was J. T. in that hallway. I had been responsible for safety on that day, and I had failed one of the dearest souls in the world, and I had to tell him. He wept, and was focused on nothing else but you.

J. T. had been told I might not live, but upon arriving in the intensive care unit later that first night, my first words to him gave great hope.

"Did you bring my makeup?" I asked. I thought if I could just make myself look better everybody would quit worrying.

The first few days in Lawton however, were touch and go, but I had no awareness of that. I was in ICU and on morphine for the pain. I also assumed the broken bones would heal and I'd be just as good as new.

The doctors had cautioned my husband not to be too optimistic, because so much could still go wrong. They were surprised I had not died from the sheer trauma of the fall or been left paralyzed, but until my vital signs stabilized they could not put me under an anesthetic to determine the extent of internal injuries.

I was later told a fall from that height could have easily caused my bladder to burst, the spleen to rupture and the broken bones to puncture my lungs.

None of that happened, just many, many broken bones and a massive hematoma—a collection of blood that was forming on my right side where the blood from all the broken bones began to pool in the hip area. I remember thinking it looked like an oversized basketball.

I later wrote in my journal that the hospital staff was concerned that small clots of blood could break loose and start traveling. As I understand it, if one lodged in my heart or lungs, I could have died, and my husband was told that one of the warning signs of a blood clot was depression. Months later, he told me that four days after the fall, as he was getting ready to leave me late one evening, I started crying.

I told him I was scared and depressed and begged him not to go. He only went as far as the nurses' station to alert the staff. I can still remember my relief when he returned to my bedside.

The medical team was afraid a clot was moving, but around two a.m., I finally quieted and slept. I have no recollection of that evening, nor how scary it must have been for J.T.

While the doctors and nurses and my family and friends knew the frightening side of what was transpiring, I remember only the good things—the gentle care of the nursing staff, the visits, cards, flowers and prayers of people who loved me.

I also received countless cards from people in Lawton churches who assured me they were praying for me too. These were men and women I did not know and would never meet, but church people were no strangers to me. I'd grown up amongst them as the preacher's kid.

For six weeks following the accident, my home was a hospital room. First in Lawton for two weeks and then when the doctors felt I could be safely moved, I was flown by air ambulance to Shawnee Medical Center in the city where I lived.

Upon my arrival by ambulance from the local airstrip, I remember being greeted by Dr. T. A. Balan, an orthopedic surgeon and a family friend. My husband and I played tennis with him and his wife, Marilyn. I knew I was in good hands.

I quickly began to rely on his care and the care of the nurses who tended me. One of my friends, RN Susan Ward, worked the night shift and spent many long nights with me watching over me. I will always be grateful for the safety I felt with her presence.

I cannot believe anyone anywhere received better care than I experienced. To the nursing staff, the crew in the surgical operating rooms, the rehabilitation specialists, and to Dr. Balan, go my profound gratitude.

I wrote in my journal that when I was finally discharged, Dr. Balan said to me, "I have seen people who were not hurt nearly as badly as you, and they didn't live." When I asked why he thought that was, he said, "Oh, I just call it the X factor."

Whatever the reason, I am still here many years later, telling you my story.

Hope: A More Gentle Name for Fear

Life is change. Growth is optional. Choose wisely.

—Karen Kaiser Clark

After arriving in the Shawnee hospital, I was immediately inundated with visitors—friends from the community, members of my church family and a multitude of college students from OBU, whose campus was just across the street from Shawnee Medical Center.

I wrote in my journal that because of the heavy pain medication I was taking, I would often reach the end of the day exhausted by the steady trek of visitors. In order to discourage this, nurses on the floor posted a sign on the door, which read "No Visitors. Family Only." College students took one look at that sign and walked right on in! We had become family and many of them are still in contact with me today.

One letter I received was from students David and Cindy Crim, who wrote: "God uses these times to teach us many lessons." And so I began to pay attention, to notice, to write them down in a journal.

Headlines in the local paper had read "40-year-old woman falls off cliff." I noted in my journal that people who knew me did not want to forget the "miracle" of my survival.

Because it was framed this way, in the months that followed I began to receive invitations to speak about my accident to churches and community groups.

Visiting with my pastor one day, I told him how uncomfortable I thought I would be to do this. There didn't seem to be a lot to tell. "I fell. I was broken. I survived." That was the story, and what I felt most was embarrassed. After all, if you're going to back off a 125-foot cliff you should be the last one to check your gear.

My pastor Dr. Dan Cooper suggested that instead of just reporting what had happened, I might want to talk about what I was *learning* from what had happened to me. It was a suggestion that shaped my recovery and changed the way I would henceforth look at life's unexpected interruptions.

Before I began writing this book, I re-read my journals and I found much I'd forgotten—people and happenings that surely affected my recovery.

There was the afternoon local dentist Grady Bowers came walking into my hospital room. My husband and I played tennis with Grady and his wife Shirley and, trying to make light of my situation, I said to him, "Well, Grady, think I should have stayed on the tennis court?"

He surprised me when in a soft voice he said, "Oh, I don't know, Charlotte. You have to think about all the hundreds of hours and dozens of kids you've spent doing these kinds of activities with—before this accident ever happened—and decide if it was worth it."

Looking at it that way, I could honestly say, "Grady, I think it may have been worth it."

"Then you've already got it beat," he told me.

A week later, into my hospital room came former OBU students Tom Westbrook, Paula Rader, Chip Anderson and Jan Tipton and my two daughters, Krista and Jayna. They announced they had come to have a worship service with me.

Tom had written a monologue that he performed, titled "Sunday Always Comes After Friday." (The resurrection always follows the crucifixion; the light always follows the darkness.) And then we sang Horatio Spafford's hymn:

> When peace like a river, attendeth my
> way, when sorrows like sea billows rolls,
> whatever my lot, Thou has taught me to
> say, it is well, it is well, with my soul.

After they left, I wrote a prayer in my journal,

> • Thank you for the Fridays and the in-be-
> tween times, so I can appreciate the Sundays
> in my life.

And without realizing it, I had put it in perspective. This was not my entire life—it was just one chapter.

Months later, in reading back over my journal, I began to gain some insight into myself. I am a person who remembers selectively. I hang on to the good and tend to minimize or forget the difficult times. I always see the glass as half full, not half empty. That may sound noble, but in reality, the glass is both.

I eventually came to understand it is important to remember the hard times as well as the good ones; that it is in the unexpected, painful, life-changing events, when "empty" is all we feel, where we find important gifts and lessons that shape the way we look at loss for the rest of our lives.

The difficult times have helped me connect to other people who are on their own journey through brokenness, much better than telling them how wonderful my life is.

Some of my journal entries give a glimpse into my darkness—the times I felt afraid, helpless and inadequate, as well as my tendency to always put on a brave front regardless of how much pain I am in. Here are some of my entries from that time:

> • I'm bored, fighting depression; wanting to take pills I don't need so I can just sleep. It is "the pits" to really want to be down and know how to keep from it!

> • I am having trouble dealing with the pain. Dr. Balan told me today I needed to get back on the crutches for the support they provide, said I was causing unnecessary problems by not using them. I feel angry and sorry for myself. I want to cry. I am ashamed that I am not handling my feelings better.

• I feel down, depressed and so weary of all the limitations.

• I love it that people want to come visit me, but by evening I am exhausted, nauseated, my legs are cramping and it is hard to keep my best face on and tell everyone I'm just fine. But I can't think of anything worse than having people feel sorry for me or see me as an invalid, so I keep on pretending everything is easy and going well.

• Because I survived, people tell me how special I am. I heard the same thing as the preacher's kid. To be special scares me. I'm afraid of making mistakes.

• I'm afraid of drawing attention to myself. People seem to need heroes, but I don't want to be one.

• I hate my disfigured foot! It's ugly! I hate the accident! I'm angry, frustrated, handicapped! And helpless to change it!

• I am exhausted.

• I feel pressure from others, paranoia, I want to quit, withdraw. I'm tired. I resent everyone who needs me. I feel guilty, inadequate, and angry.

And then the journal entry that set light bulbs going off in my brain, written a year following the accident:

> • I have begun walking every evening at the OBU track. Yesterday I wondered if I could run. Then I hesitated. What if someone saw me? Even though the pain would never be gone, they might think it was and believe I was completely okay. I didn't run long.

> • The thoughts that went running through my head as I drove home were that "the accident is over and becomes past tense when I start jogging. I won't get any more attention or sympathy."

Later I wrote:

> • I always tell people I'm a tough lady, but with no crisis in my world I think I'll feel empty.

> • Is giving up the pain so difficult? Is walking away from my tough luck so hard? Is leaving my crutch behind such a reluctant act? Has that become my identity? My attention-getter?

> • Sounds sick. Sounds familiar. I hear it all the time in my office. "I can't change because my parents were bad." "I can't help how I feel because I was abused." "That's the way I

am…I am alone." "I can't do it because I am afraid."

· And in working so hard to hang on to the familiar pain and brokenness, people pass up chances to re-channel energy needed to use in looking for alternatives and discovering new paths toward growth.

· I am beginning to see that for myself the old familiar paths keep me in a rut and I get bored with myself, which leads to feeling inadequate. What in all of our lives do we need to learn from and then let go? Why is that so difficult? Why so scary? Does it matter that I under-stand—or just accept and act!

Helpful Hands, Loving Hearts

> Each person grows not only by her own talents
> and development of her inner beliefs, but also
> by what she receives from the persons around
> her.
>
> —Iris Haberli

Re-reading those journal entries, I see how easy it is to get stuck in the brokenness. It becomes a way to be special, a way to get attention, a way to excuse ourselves from responsibility.

I also discovered the journal writings had been a dialogue with God. One request to Him that I would find over and over and over in those early pages was,

> • Since this has happened, please don't let it be misused and please don't let it be wasted.

I was afraid of the accident being "misused" because

at the age of forty and the height from which I'd fallen, it was surprising I'd survived and the college students who'd been with me that day were telling people that my survival was a "miracle."

I do remember the helicopter circling and students sounding frustrated because it was not lowering into the canyon. I also remember it clouding over and their concern that it might rain and someone creating a makeshift tent over my body.

The part I don't remember is that after the sound of thunder, the sun was covered over with clouds rolling in and the temperature dropped about ten degrees.

As the helicopter lifted off, the students asked the solders who had to wait behind what had taken so long for them to get down into the canyon. Students later explained to me what they understood. Because of the narrow walls of the canyon, the 110 degree temperature and the aerodynamics of a helicopter, the pilot was afraid when they tried to lift off a vacuum would be created and there could possibly be a problem getting out of the canyon.

A vacuum? Tom Westbrook later explained this to me:

> The temperature was dropping in the advance of the thunderstorms, but again, that is a tradeoff with increasing humidity and a dropping barometric pressure. Those made it as if the chopper was flying at a much higher altitude. Harder to get lift. Harder to control. The chopper's downdraft in that little valley made its own weather—thus the student's 'vacuum' expression.

Students went on to tell that apparently the decision had been made to return to the base, get equipment to lower a stretcher and hoist me up to the top and load me in from there, when it clouded over and the temperature dropped ten degrees. The soldiers said, "That's when we came in and got her out."

"A miracle," the students insisted. Others seemed to have no trouble believing it, but I soon discovered I was very uncomfortable with it. I believed God was with me through it all, but while I believe in miracles, I am not a person who needs miracles to believe. Besides, what about all those folks who have prayed for a miracle and didn't get it?

My dad taught me when we experience an act of good fortune, it is right to give thanks, but he did not think it was right to claim special status with God as a reason. So I found I was more comfortable just thinking of what had happened to me as an accident, much like other people suffer in automobile crashes or falls on the ski slopes.

Was it a miracle? I still do not know if it was—and it still does not matter. If it was, I am humbled and grateful.

The other part of my prayer—"don't let it be wasted"—simply meant that since it had happened, I wanted it to be useful. That became clear very quickly because the lessons I learned were many. Some of them I could have learned another way, but this was the experience that would teach me.

As an only child, I was adept at taking care of myself, but through that time of brokenness, when for the first three weeks I could only move my arms and nothing else,

I realized I couldn't go it alone, and at age forty I learned to rely on others.

I experienced the warmth and care of my church family. Shawnee First Baptist Church members not only prayed for me, they cleaned my house, fed my family and mowed my yard. They stayed in touch and became my best cheerleaders in the months of recovery that were to follow.

Giving for me had always been easy, but I came to understand the importance of being a good receiver— one of the most gracious things you can do in response to a gift of any kind.

Cards and flowers and personal items arrived daily. I loved them all, but one gift that will forever stand out in my memory was a package from Bobby Rose, a member of our college group. I was still in the Lawton hospital when I opened the package to find a children's book, *The Giving Tree*, by Shel Silverstein.

Bobby knew I collected children's books. He also knew I had this particular book and I wondered why he would send me something I already owned. And then I opened the inside front cover and read, "I thought while you were in the hospital, you might like to have some-thing to give away."

At a time when I was almost completely immobile, needing even the simplest tasks done for me, it allowed me the opportunity to feel useful, to have something to offer. Before I left Lawton to return to Shawnee, I gave the book to Janet Kenyan, a nurse who'd spent many hours with me during the long nights. It was a way for me to say *thank you* for the care and the friendship she'd offered.

Because of Bobby's gift, I shall forever believe it is blessed to give—and to receive—and important to do both well.

Limitations, Laughter and Leaps

Continuity gives us roots; change gives us branches, letting us stretch and grow and reach new heights.

—Pauline R. Kezer

Another insight came that would help me understand my parents as they aged.

When it came time for me to leave the hospital and return home, I found myself apprehensive and concerned. I knew my husband and our children had gone through a difficult period with my absence. A line in a note from my youngest daughter had given me a clue. She wrote:

My insides are frozen. I am afraid. I want to cry, to fall apart. It is so darned frustrating at home without you. The house isn't the same house. Even the cats act different.

From these four people, who before the accident depended on me to be the strong one, I was going to be needing a lot of tending and care. I was afraid of becoming a burden to those I loved the most.

Therefore as my parents aged and needed more assistance, I was able to understand their apologies when they asked for help and how much they hated "being a bother."

I also gained a bit of insight into what it must be like to be handicapped. While spending months in a cast, in a wheelchair and on crutches, I came to realize that not only strangers, but also people who knew me well, talked down to me as if I were a child. It was as though something had happened to my mind as well as my body.

I was speaking about this one day to a college student who was blind. He told me most people passed by him without speaking because they thought he wouldn't know they were there.

Even if we don't want to believe it, most of us are uncomfortable with disabilities. This has been incredibly helpful to me and now when I encounter someone who is obviously handicapped in some way, I make eye contact and I speak to them as adults and with respect.

And what would we do without laughter? Studies have been done that show it is helpful in the healing process. Laughter came to me in many forms.

A cartoon that came in the mail featured a picture of a climbing instructor on the side of a cliff with a group of students. As one of them falls, the instructor leans over and yells to him on his way down, "You get flunked for that!"

My friend Tom Westbrook coming to see me in the hospital and telling me, "When they finally loaded you into the helicopter I am sure your guardian angel leaned up against the cliff and looking toward heaven said, "Dear

God, would you please let me trade her in for someone else? She's wearing me out!"

And then there was the letter from Kentucky from my friend Brack Marquette. Brack was an OBU professor who had grown up in Kentucky and was home visiting his mother for the summer. His letter arrived shortly after my return to Shawnee.

Most letters I received began with "I've been praying for you," which I deeply appreciated. This letter, however, opened with "Dear Charlotte, I hear you fell and busted your ass!"

My father would never have believed an OBU professor would talk like that. It caught me by such surprise that I can remember laughing out loud. When I later told my friend Jan Greene about his opening line, she commented, "Sounds like he knew you well enough to have confidence in your ability to laugh at yourself." Another gift that I'd not realized. I like knowing people might see me that way.

While laughter is healing, I learned that words said without thinking can get in the way, because you hear them differently when you are broken. And I began to realize that in our desire to comfort, we should be more thoughtful about the words we use, particularly those of us who are Christians.

An aunt who is now deceased wrote to me, "God works in mysterious ways to slow us down when we get too busy." I remember looking at her letter and wondering if she really thought God had pushed me over that cliff.

Another person asked if I ever thought God was punishing me. It never dawned on me. I do not believe in a God who wants to hurt His children.

The implication that God was responsible for my accident was never a helpful thought. But could He use what had happened to me? I certainly hoped so.

Yet when the letter came that said, "God must have great things for you to do," I did not find it comforting. With all the broken bones, unable to care for myself, and needing assistance with the smallest things, *great things to do* felt overwhelming.

But I gave it thought. Eventually I decided that God is just not so desperate that He must push people off cliffs so they can do great things. In fact, I think He has great plans for all of us and if we are not there to do them, He will simply offer the opportunity to someone else.

And with that realization I now look back and understand my spiritual growth just took a big leap. I went from a naïve child believing everything depended on my being the example for the whole world to a more mature adult woman who realized I am no more important to this world than anyone else. I can take the opportunities that come to me, or not. Someone else will step up and do it if I say no, and I will not be loved less.

The big "Aha!" moment was the understanding that God's work never depends on just one person. So whatever I do now, I do for the sheer joy of doing it, not because if I don't do it, it won't get done.

Another gift was a bible verse, II Corinthians 12:9, which often came to mind during those days when I was not physically strong and needed much help:

> But he said to me, My grace is sufficient for you,
> for my power is made perfect in weakness.

I feel certain the scripture verses I'd learned as a child

were a big reason I do not remember ever being afraid following the accident. There was an incredible certainty that my Heavenly Father was with me and whatever lay ahead, He would be present and would give me the strength I needed to face it. I also believed there would come a time when I would walk out into the sunlight again, intact, although changed forever.

The "changed forever" part was realized when I accepted there was some pain that might never go away. Mine happened to be physical. For others it is emotional or mental or relational. But there are times when all you can do is learn to tend the pain well. To ignore it will only cause more problems, as I would soon discover.

I learned from author Michael Drury that the opposite of courage is not so much fear, but laziness, indifference, discouragement, defeat, cynicism, pessimism, "un-courage" so to speak. I realized I could complain and whine or I could learn new skills, adjust to the changes, practice different behaviors and get used to the way things were now.

The "now," I realized, held limitations—the need to ask for help, the inability to go for long without resting, as well as all the feelings I was not well acquainted with that came along with the new experiences.

I gradually learned when I try to ignore the feelings and keep them inside and hidden, I rob myself of the ability to make decisions and to see the problem clearly. It really does help to share them with someone else.

And then for the first time, I came face to face with the fragility of life. I realized I could die before I was old. I have no recollection that the awareness frightened me, but it did bring a determination to live each day well. To do that, I needed to understand that while I will always miss what I have lost, I can still make today a good day.

Encouragement Is a Wonderful Thing

> It's gonna be a long hard drag, but we'll make it.
>
> —Janis Joplin

Words are powerful. They can hurt. They can also heal.

Healing words came to me from a variety of people of all ages and backgrounds.

From a high school teacher who had my daughters in class came a plaque, which read "Blessed are the curious, for they shall have adventures." Being aware that many adults saw my rappelling as something foolish, I deeply appreciated his reframing it as an adventure. At least in his eyes, I was curious rather than stupid.

Then of course, there were the college students who began to speak of my accident as "our accident." It prompted me to write in my journal, "...guess I've got company to proceed in *our* recovery."

Gene Rainbolt, president of BancFirst in Shawnee

at the time, came to visit. Before leaving he said, "I've been concerned, but I believe in you and that you will be whole because you are Charlotte."

A note from Mrs. Forsythe, an elderly lady in a nursing home who I had chatted with a few times when visiting my grandmother, said "Great things come to one who has courage. You have it dear. I don't forget to pray for you."

From my son Bart, who told me, "People were telling Dad you might die. I never believed it."

Four notes came from Mrs. Opal Craig—a retired professor of speech at OBU and my teacher in Speech 101 when I was an eighteen-year-old college freshman. I am sharing them with you to give you an idea of words that can be helpful. I have used some of them over the years, when writing to someone else in a dark time. Opal would be delighted to know you might find them useful also.

Opal's First Note

> Dear Charlotte,
>
> I was having my quiet prayer before I got out of bed this morning because I had awakened thinking of you. As I thought of the pain that has been your constant companion, my mind went to another friend who has had surgery several times and other occasions of intense pain. She says she just takes her mind and moves it far, far away from the pain and thinks long, lovely thoughts. Maybe you can make that work for you. I am constantly holding you close.
>
> Love,
> Opal

Opal's Second Note

Dear Charlotte,

I came gently awake at 6 a.m. for a brief visit with you, beginning with the cute Charlotte Perkins in Speech 101—over on the north side, I think in the first row—though many years since. To know her has always been sheer joy.

Here's a little four-liner I've kept and loved for years. Join me in its therapy:

Not for one single day,
Can I discern my way.
Who gives the day, will show the way.
So, I serenely go.

Love,
Opal

Opal's Third Note (written on Saturday, July 14, 1979)

Dear Charlotte,

Well, we both made it through Friday the 13th, didn't we?

Here's another quotation from which I have gathered strength on many occasions. Try it on for size: I said to the man who stood at the gate of the year, "Give me light that I may tread softly into the unknown," and he said, "Go into the darkness and put your hand into the hand of God, and this to you will be better than the light and safer than the known way."

My good thoughts and prayers continue as well as my love.

Opal

Opal's Fourth Note

Dear Charlotte,

My morning devotional for today is Isaiah 30: *And therefore will the Lord wait, that He may be gracious unto you—blessed are all they that wait for Him.* Waiting in the sunshine of His love is what will ripen the soul for His blessing.

When I waked at 6 a.m., as always, I rushed—in space—to your bedside to hold your hand. We reaffirmed the fact that you and I are in the center of His will. With His help we can handle today.

I think I've told you before that for some strange reason, you are with me much of the time. I lift you in prayer many times a day. I'm beginning to understand now. It is from you I gain strength. Through your patient suffering I am learning. So see, your influence from Shawnee Medical Center room 321 is still a force.

I'm looking forward to the time someone can come by and take me to see you. Remember I am holding you close.

Much Love,
Opal

There were the words of wisdom from Rev. Francis Broyles, a retired minister and member of my church family, who wrote to me: "Maybe you will find there are spiritual heights and plateaus that take a lot more courage and stamina than conquering a mountain—and are far more rewarding." And of course he was right.

And then there were the moments when no words at all were spoken or necessary. One incident had to do with my son Bart. During the weeks after my return home from the hospital, Bart would enter the house every afternoon, head for my bedroom to sit beside me and tell me about his day.

Bart can make anything sound like an adventure, and I can remember we laughed a lot. And then there was the day Bart was standing at the foot of my bed, demonstrating a powerful tennis swing that had just won him a match. On the downswing, the racket accidentally caught a part of my damaged foot. I must have screamed in pain—that I don't remember. What I do recall is Bart crawling up beside me in bed and holding on tightly while we cried together.

And then there was the moment with my friend, Dot Gorley. Dot was a member of the staff at First Baptist Church in Shawnee and also worked with me in the ministry to college students. Any time we went away on a retreat, Dot went along to cook for us. Her home-cooked meals were always the highlight of the trip.

A week following the accident, Dot drove to Lawton on a Saturday morning. She entered my hospital room and without saying a word walked over to me and carefully put her arms around my shoulders, the only part of me that was not broken, laid her cheek next to mine and wept.

Bart and Dot's tenderness and tears were as profound as any words that could have been written or spoken.

Pain, A Constant Companion

There are two ways of meeting difficulties.
You alter the difficulties or you alter yourself
to meet them.

—Phyliss Bottome

I did not know until years later how much I would need
what I had learned from that accident. As I journeyed
through the rest of my life, there were going to be other
broken times and other losses ahead.

I now see there are many ways to be broken. My
accident was physical. There are also financial and emotional and spiritual breaks. There are relationships that
cannot be put back together and careers that cannot be
regained.

There are terminal illnesses and impending death that
will tear families apart, and children in trouble that leave
families fragmented.

What I began to realize was that because I had gone

through the helplessness and pain of a broken time, that experience in the future would serve as a bridge from me to other people who were going through their own dark times.

While my easy, simple early life had been difficult for hurting people to identify with, my broken body and the constant physical pain made me someone they could trust and believed could understand.

This has served me well as a therapist, possibly as much as the educational degree. I may be more credible because I've been there. I am not only a counselor, I am also a fellow struggler and far more compassionate.

Never content to lie in bed for long, or enjoy being sick, I was willing to push and get out of the house and back into some ordinary routines just a few weeks after leaving the hospital.

Still in a cast, needing a wheelchair and always with back pain, I traveled with my husband to Providence, Rhode Island, in September to enroll our oldest daughter, Krista, in Brown University.

From my wheelchair I was on campus to greet OBU students who were returning to campus for the fall semester. This was important to me because I had accepted a part-time position as director of Student Ministries at First Baptist Church just prior to the accident.

Never having been employed before, even part-time, and already in love with college students, I think that new challenge was key in my working hard to not let casts and crutches and wheelchairs keep me from being involved in living.

Besides it was work where I could take my two younger kids, Jayna and Bart, right along with me. They too made many friends from among the college crowd.

OBU was only a few miles from our church. 1979 was a time when few students had cars. We sent a church bus to the campus several times a week to bring students to the church for worship and other activities.

In addition, I spent many hours on the OBU campus, hanging out in the Student Union, attending campus activities and taking students to lunch. It was an opportunity that turned out to be one of the great joys of my life.

My goal in working with students was to give them a safe place to explore their faith, provide opportunities to express that faith in creative ways and encourage them to be a "real" person, no pretense.

To be part of our group meant coming with your fears, questions and imperfections, and knowing you would not be judged. You would be loved just as you were, warts and all. Since some of my physical imperfections were quite obvious, it was a nice fit.

While I knew it was important to teach and educate and give them opportunities for service in the church and the community, I also knew it was important to play. College students need a break from studies, and working and playing together helps in growing friendships and building a sense of community.

Even though the back pain was my constant friend, I refused to let it limit me and I traveled with students on mission trips, campouts and weekend retreats. We skied Colorado mountain slopes in the winter and floated in rafts down the Illinois River during the spring and summer. Anywhere we traveled with those young men and women, we ate well. Dot wouldn't have it any other way.

With family members, I traveled inside the United

States and also to Scotland and to the Bahamas, to Paris and London, to West Berlin, East Berlin, and other places behind the Iron Curtain.

A favorite we all remember was a trip to New Orleans that J.T., Jayna, Bart and I made. We still laugh about my first time on Bourbon Street in a cast and a wheelchair. As my chair would roll past the pimps and the hustlers in front of the clubs, they turned into perfect gentlemen, quickly stepping forward to assist us if the chair needed to be lifted on or off a curb.

When Jayna tells the story, she always adds, "Mom was just a little bit hurt that no one seemed to make passes at ladies in wheelchairs!"

All the traveling came about because I had decided if I had to live with constant pain, then I would just take it along. If I was going to hurt, regardless of where I was, then I might as well go ahead and have some adventures.

While that sounds noble and brave, the problem was I would try to ignore the pain rather than respect it and manage it. And I nearly always reached a point where it became out of control and landed me flat on my back. Rather than learn from it, I chafed against it.

Many a doctor and physical therapist said to me, "You must pay attention to your pain. It is your friend because it is telling you there's something you need to take care of. It may mean you need to stop and rest awhile, or simply slow down and take breaks, or perhaps make some permanent changes." I didn't want to hear that.

Funny thing about pain—sometimes you can get so used to it that having it becomes normal. Years later, I see that perhaps that is why we can stay too long in places and situations that hurt us. We forget there is any other way to live.

During the months that followed the accident, Dr. Balan had often reminded me that there were times when I needed to pick up the crutches again because I was making things worse—just a simple acknowledgement that I needed some help.

I have met many folks since then who, like me, find that difficult to do. It feels like a sign of weakness. Old habits are hard to break because no one ever taught us that being aware you need help—and then asking for it—takes great courage.

A Failure for Everyone to See

People change and forget to tell each other.
—Lillian Hellman

My first experience of brokenness and pain beyond my control was physical. But ten years later I would come face to face with another. This one was a broken relationship.

As sometimes happens, my husband and I had gotten busy with jobs and different interests and found ourselves going in different directions. And then there is the growing up and maturing that often happens after you get married. The young man or woman you are in your early twenties may be very different from who you are twenty-five years later.

My marriage of thirty years was in trouble. The word divorce had been mentioned. In the home where I was raised, that was seen as a failure. In the churches where I was raised as a child, that was not seen as a viable option.

A few journal entries from that time:

> • I am tired. Confused...I can help others, but not myself.

> • There is a restlessness in me that is unsettling. Sometimes the feeling of dread just creeps over me.

As the emotional pain grew larger, so did the physical pain.

More journal entries:

> • There is increasing back pain. What do I do? I don't want to complain, call attention to it, be whiny, but it doesn't let up. I'm scared no doctor will ever be able to help me.

> • Time management and pain management go together for me. So why am I surprised when the pain is out of control when I have not stopped to take care of myself?

> • In spite of the pain medication, my back is knotting up because I don't seem to be able to stop and rest. When will I ever learn?

> • Physical pain gets worse. Dr. Balan injected anti-inflammatory medicine right into the sacrum area today. It is swollen and very pain-

ful. Once again, I have waited until the pain
was impossible to ignore. Why do I do that?

Looking back on those journal entries, I realize that
acknowledging pain was seen as a weakness for me. If
I wouldn't acknowledge physical pain, I should not be
surprised I did not let anyone know about the emotional
pain of a marriage in trouble.

Later, I would ask myself why I felt it necessary to
keep any problems hidden from my friends and family.
And then I remembered an incident with my father when
I was in grade school. He came home one day following a
funeral and said to my mother, "Can you believe the way
that woman carried on?"

As an adult, I know that preachers are human, too,
and there were times when I saw my dad tired and
exhausted and used up. It was probably one of those
days. In hindsight, I see that his remarks to my mother
served like a debriefing. He would never have thought
someone shouldn't cry when a loved one died. On the
other hand, I know he was uncomfortable with public
displays of grief, as are many folks.

But as a young daughter who always wanted to please
her daddy, I heard it just as he said it and I think I must
have decided I would never be a woman who "carried
on." As a result, while I seem to be comfortable with others expressing painful emotions, it is often difficult for
me to do the same for myself.

And then another light bulb went on when I read a
journal entry written a year later.

> • A habit left over from childhood—I see that I
> look at people who matter to me, try to figure
> out what they want me to be, then try to be

that...even when it means shoving aside my own needs.

And just as I had ignored the pain of my physical body, I had ignored the seriousness of the pain in my marriage. In the same way that I had plunged into work with students to ignore the physical pain, I had also used my work with them as an escape from the problems at home.

I wanted people to believe I was the perfect wife and the perfect parent, and now everybody was going to know it wasn't true. I might not be in a wheelchair, but I would be "divorced." Broken. And, once again, everyone would see.

I had been an "over-functioner" deluxe. I thought I could fix anything and anybody. It wasn't true. Many of the same feelings from the accident surfaced. Helpless. Ashamed. Embarrassed. I didn't want anyone to know I needed help, when the truth was, it was clear to everyone but me.

From this fear of being known, I now see the only person I was really deceiving was myself. I was staying in pain—emotional pain this time—because I was afraid to admit my failures and ask for help. I wonder whom I thought that blessed? Certainly not myself, and I doubt anyone else.

Once again I found myself at the bottom. Not the bottom of a canyon this time, but the bottom of a marriage, with no idea of what the future would hold. And once again, with great reluctance, I finally got around to asking for help.

I wrote in my journal, "Can I need help and still be wonderful?" Reminded me of the day at the OBU track, wondering if I was no longer an accident victim, would I still be special?

At the same time the emotional pain was nearing out-of-control status, the physical pain was becoming worse as well. My badly injured back was screaming for attention. Another round of second opinions, however, brought good news—and bad news. The good news was surgeons did not want to fuse the back joints. The bad news was "it will get worse." I slowly began to realize the same thing about my marriage.

Again, I was being forced to face the pain so I could manage it—all of the pain, and at the age of fifty, my marriage of thirty years ended in divorce.

I later began to realize that I was so steeped in my own pain, I didn't understand how the divorce was affecting my children. There would no longer be "home" to go to. There would be two separate residences, both unfamiliar, both holding hurting parents who wanted to talk about their own pain and explain their side of the story in order to justify their actions. The children did not want to take sides, and it must have felt as though we were both asking for that.

Right after I filed for divorce, it felt like my three adult children distanced from me. I wanted to explain. I wanted to be understood. They didn't want to hear. I wrote in my journal, "I feel abandoned by my children."

Slowly but surely our children have found their way back to each of us and now we share not only children, but eight grandchildren as well. Jessica and Sarah, Aly and Sebastian, Jacob and Zachary, Erin and Ryan.

Through the divorce and the months that followed, no one needed to tell me to write in a journal. I filled volumes. And looking back, I once again found the lessons, the gifts.

As before, my church family prayed for me and wrapped their arms around me. My friends Margaret Davis, Dot and Joe Gorley, Pam and Matt Goree, Max Brattin, and Patsy and Reid Hutchens listened to me and hugged me and reminded me I still mattered.

I began to understand I had to quit expecting someone else to make me happy. That was my responsibility.

I embraced Paul Harvey's definition of success: I get up when I fall down.

I learned patience is not a feeling, but a way of behaving when I am full of anxiety.

I realized forgiving myself was as important as forgiving another person.

And I learned that when one life ends, another is waiting.

What I had tried to teach college students was tested. I had told them that I believe in a God who not only creates us, but loves us, gifts us, and does not abandon us when we fail, but forgives us, offers us a second chance and guides us into a new path—changed forever, and maybe scarred, but intact and useful.

I now understand that belief was instilled in me by my parents and the churches who nurtured me in those first eighteen years of my life. It has been enough to see me through some dark times and has kept me putting one foot in front of the other. What I still did not fully grasp was how my divorce could be used to help other people in their own time of pain, but I believed it possible.

The scripture verse that surfaced in my head over and over and over was Jeremiah 29:11:

For surely I know the plans I have for you, says the LORD, plans for your welfare and not for harm, to give you a future with hope.

Life Is Never Settled

Adventure is worthwhile in itself.

—Amelia Earhart

And sure enough, in my fifties I found some new "firsts."

I entered my first full-time job as a marketing director for Oak Crest Psychiatric hospital, a private in-patient mental health facility for children and adults, located on the outskirts of Shawnee.

I adopted a son. Alan Parker was thirty-one years old, I was fifty-two. I had met Alan as a student at OBU in 1980, when he'd been twenty years old. Both of his parents had died before he graduated from high school. He simply had no extended family, and I had taken him home with me.

Alan had been with our family for holidays and summers for many years. One evening as I was thinking about him, I wondered why we had never legally adopted him. It seems to me everyone deserves to belong to somebody. And then I had a glorious thought! Why not now?

I called my adult children to run the idea by them. No problem there. I called California, where Alan was currently living. I only remember soft weeping—his, then mine, then ours together.

May 1, 1992, we made it official. Alan came from California. My friend Fred came from New Orleans, my son Bart from Fort Worth, my mother and my friend Margaret from across town.

My daughters were both out of the country, but they sent "Welcome to the Family" messages. My friends sent flowers saying, "Congratulations, it's a boy," and I strung a banner across the front of my house that read "Welcome Home."

In one afternoon, I went from mother of three to mother of four, and Alan got a mother, a grandmother, sisters, a brother, nieces and nephews.

During that time I also completed requirements for licensure as a marriage and family therapist and moved to Oklahoma City where I was hired as assistant director of Baptist Medical Center's Outpatient Counseling Center.

Dr. Bill Carpenter, who served as director of Pastoral Care at the hospital, also oversaw the counseling center, and he wanted me to be in charge of two things. He wanted me to serve as a part-time therapist, and he also wanted me to market the center so we could raise our visibility, hire more therapists and serve more people.

Going to work at the same time for Dr. Carpenter was Kerry Ann Richards, the person who ran the office and fielded the phone calls and made everyone who came to the Center feel like they'd come into a happy and very safe place. She and I still work together, and she has become one of my most treasured friends and co-workers.

During the next two years, we all worked hard. We hired more therapists, moved to larger office space and served hundreds of people who found themselves at a crossroads.

One mother I met who was at a crossroads was Sondra Woodruff, mother of nine-year-old Jason and seventeen-year-old Jenni. Her husband had died three months before.

Jason had seen a television program about The Dougy Center in Portland, Oregon, that provided support groups for kids who had had a family member die. It has been started by a friend of Dr. Kubler-Ross. Jason wanted to know if there was a place like that for him in Oklahoma City.

His mother began to make phone calls, making inquiries about grief support groups for children. One day she placed a call to Oklahoma City's Baptist Medical Center and the call was sent over to my office.

I was new to the Oklahoma City area in 1992 and was not yet well acquainted with those kinds of resources, but I told her I was sure there was something out there and I would help her find it. Soon we discovered there was no ongoing program like this in our community, so I made a phone call to The Dougy Center, asking if we could start a Dougy Center in our city. The answer was no, but they would offer training and share materials and then we could shape a group that would fit our needs and choose our own name.

They referred me for training to one of their training

centers in Fort Worth. That center is called The Warm Place.

Jason's Mom and I went to The Warm Place for a weekend's training and then I came back to Oklahoma City and called *The Oklahoman.* I asked if they would do a story about the support groups that would allow us to make a plea for volunteers who would undergo special training and serve as facilitators of the groups.

The Oklahoman sent staff writer Bernice McShane, a lady who listened carefully to my story about the importance of providing support and a safe place for kids to talk and to learn new ways of coping as they moved through grief.

In a soft voice Bernice turned to me and said to me, "I understand. My mother died when I was four, and I went to live with my grandmother. She died when I was eight, and I did not begin to deal with my grief until I was in my fifties." You will not be surprised to know her story brought us a special group of volunteers.

When Jason and I talked about what we would name our children's grief support groups, he told me the story of sailing with his father:

> When we would be out on the lake and the winds were high and the waters choppy, I would be really scared sometimes. But then we would sail into the harbor where the waters were calm and I'd feel safe again.

And so Calm Waters was born. Judy Mee followed me as Executive Director, and it was under her leadership that the program today is a freestanding non-profit organization, still in the business of helping families, offering both grief and divorce groups for kids from three to eighteen. When Judy retired, Donna Lawrence became director, followed by Barbara Butner. The groups are facilitated by a group of dedicated, trained volunteers under the leadership of an educated and talented staff.

At the same time I was involved in my job, I was continuing to see a therapist and work on myself. I was divorced and that brought a new set of challenges—where do I go from here and what happens next? Before I could look forward, a suggestion from my therapist was to look back and find those folks who, as I was growing up, had made a significant contribution to my life, to locate them, and tell them thank you.

One of the persons on my list was my childhood friend Fred Lankard, who I discovered was currently living in New Orleans, Louisiana. We had lived next door to one another in Kingfisher, Oklahoma, from the time we were eleven years old until we left for college. We were not only neighbors, we had been playmates, classmates and high school sweethearts.

His kindness, his laughter, his respectful acceptance of all the restrictions set by my father had left a lasting impression on me. Fred later told me he certainly had not liked the limits and never understood them, but he never said that to me and he never questioned my need to obey my dad.

I later realized he had also given me something that was similar to what I'd received from my mother. He too believed that who I was, was enough—and that I could do anything I set my mind to.

And so I wrote the letter of recognition and thanks—and received an immediate response. He was delighted to hear from me, and we talked about seeing each other at our next Kingfisher High School reunion. For some reason, we had never both been present at the same time for previous reunions.

At first there would be an occasional phone call, a letter and then he planned a visit to his mother who was in the early stages of Alzheimer's. He had asked if I was free when he came to Kingfisher, could we meet in Oklahoma City for lunch and a visit. The letters and phone calls and visits continued, and we began to fill in the years since our high school graduation in 1957.

I recall later sitting in his mother's living room, looking back over old photograph albums, seeing the many pictures of us together as teenagers—dressed up for a class dinner, in our caps and gowns ready for graduation, in jeans and shirts playing baseball on the corner lot. There was much laughter and a fun trip down memory lane as we talked of jobs and families, vacations and adventures, new experiences and ones that we regretted.

We looked further back into our teen years, remembering that after high school graduation, we had known our relationship would be over. We would attend different colleges in Oklahoma, he to the University of Oklahoma in Norman and I to Shawnee's Oklahoma Baptist University.

We had known for certain that we would eventually marry and have families, but not with each other. We knew this because my father was a conservative Southern Baptist preacher, who did not believe in mixed marriages—and Fred was a Methodist.

Fred and I discovered that we both had kept bracelets given to each other during our senior year in high school. Christmas of our senior year, he had given me a silver ID bracelet with both our names engraved on it.

And the summer before he left for college, I had given him a bracelet made out of cheap, plastic, pop-in beads, and told him if he would keep it with him he'd always be safe.

He put his bracelet into the glove compartment of his car and over the years, every time he changed cars, he'd come across that bracelet and it would go into the new glove compartment. He remembered one of his children asking one day why he kept that old thing that was dirty and worn. He said he simply smiled and said, "It brings me good luck."

The silver ID bracelet went into my jewelry box. When my youngest daughter was small, she liked to go through my jewelry and try on pieces. When she would come across that bracelet she'd ask me to tell her the story about my childhood friend. I would tell her what I remembered most about him was that he liked to laugh, he had very good manners and he was always kind.

A Time to Laugh, A Time to Mourn

I wanted a perfect ending…Now I've learned,
the hard way, that some poems don't rhyme
and some stories don't have a clear beginning,
middle and end. Life is about not knowing,
having to change, taking the moment and
making the best of it, without knowing what's
going to happen next.

—Gilda Radner

I will always remember the first time Fred and I saw each
other again after all those years. He was no longer the tall
skinny kid with lots of hair that I remembered, and I was
graying and had wrinkles, but we soon began to discover
that the friendship we had built as young children was
still intact and provided a solid foundation on which to
build a new and mature love in our later years.

And then there was the phone call from Fred from
New Orleans in January of 1993, telling me he was mov-
ing back to Oklahoma. His son, Wake, was a student at
OU and his daughter, Annie, was planning to enroll at
OU after high school graduation. This is where had he
had grown up and his family still owned several acres of

farmland in the Kingfisher area. He would enjoy being closer to his children, "the cousins," and friends he had grown up with—and closer to me.

We were married when we were fifty-three years old.

Fred and I were good partners. We cherished each day as it came. We found marriage the second time around much easier because we had learned from our mistakes.

And again, I found lessons, except this time they came from an experience that was happy and joyful.

I could read II Corinthians 13:4–7 and smile knowingly.

> Love is patient, love is kind. It does not envy, it does not boast, it is not proud. It is not rude, it is not self-seeking, it is not easily angered, it keeps no record of wrongs. Love does not delight in evil but rejoices with the truth. It always protects, always trusts, always hopes, always perseveres.

I learned that love knows where all your buttons are—and does not push them.

I learned the importance of respect and kindness in a relationship and that love *always* means saying, "I'm sorry."

I learned a marriage is simply easier when you have a lot of interests in common.

I learned to treat each day with gratitude.

I learned intimacy is not about walking beside each other to hold each other up, but it is about two strong people walking beside each other because some times it is nice to lean a little.

I learned to stay up to date with my anger, that it is

wise to never go to bed mad and that it was okay to ask for what I wanted and needed.

I learned that experiencing joy is a direct result of willingness to share each other's pain and deepest fears.

I did not make the same mistakes that I'd made as a twenty-year-old because I had learned the difference between growing older and growing up. Growing older means merely to age. Growing up means becoming wiser and better at living your life.

As all newlyweds do, we expected to live *happily ever after*, surely another twenty-five years anyway, but that was not to be. Two days before our third wedding anniversary, Fred was diagnosed with pancreatic cancer. One hundred days later, on June 11, 1996, he died.

Once again, I found myself broken, but this time I felt totally helpless to fix it and for the first time in my life, I felt hopeless.

I remember when Fred was first diagnosed with cancer I found it difficult to talk about it with anyone. The loss of what I was facing was too hard to grasp. Saying it out loud made it too real. All I wanted to do was run away. I did not want to go where I was being told I had to go.

Just like at the time of the accident and the divorce, friends again reached out. And again, I found it difficult to let anyone "see" the pain. It was probably because I did not want to face it myself. I did not want to manage it. I simply wanted to run away from it. I did not want to travel the road that was ahead of me.

At the same time, I knew our families and closest friends wanted to know how we were doing and I found it was easier to write letters. The first letter was written six weeks after his diagnosis. I wrote five more in the months that followed his death.

My friend Judy Mee, who was a therapist in my office at the time of Fred's illness and death, kept those six letters, and ten years later she returned them to me and encouraged me to share them with you. I've chosen a few paragraphs from each one.

First Letter to Judy
Six weeks after the diagnosis

Dear Judy,

Two weeks ago, Fred woke up about 3 a.m. complaining about a band of severe pain in his back that was new. He said to me, "I think this is the beginning of the end." Of course we have no way of knowing, but for him it means more morphine, which we slowly increase, which means that even if he lives, he will become less and less alert.

When anyone asks, I usually say that we are doing okay, but the truth is things are not okay at all.

In the last week, the liver has begun to malfunction. We have blood drawn every other day and the results are not good. It is as though our life has been interrupted in a way that seems too big to manage.

Friends and family are being great as they reach out with letters, cards, telegrams, flowers, visits, messages left on our answering machine, food for the freezer.

Fred particularly enjoys the visits of "the

cousins"—Pat Baldwin, Sherry Wrobbel and Diane Musick, who live in Kingfisher, and his best friend Wayne Francis. Fred and Wayne's fathers were friends. Both sons were born in the same year and have played together since they were infants.

College classmates are getting in touch, former bosses and co-workers, even both our "ex's" are writing to say they are thinking about us and have put Fred on their respective church prayer lists.

Jananne is remembering the fun times she and Fred shared with their children and the memories of him she plans to share with their grandchildren.

J.T. has let me know he's spending extra time with my mother and if I need anything, all I have to do is call.

All of the children stay in touch and visit when they can. Fred feels a great sense of pride that Wake and Annie are such great grown-ups. Like their father, I watch them embrace the moment, reach out for the adventure, and if everything does not turn out as hoped, they will learn from the experience and even have a few laughs along the way.

My four kids, plus spouses and grandchildren, are richer because of the time Fred has spent with them, although the time has been brief. For my two daughters, Fred has made a good "extra" as friend and grandparent. My youngest son, Bart acknowledges that he probably needed two dads!

For my adopted son, Alan, who is gay, Fred has been a stepfather who comfortably accepts who he is, wants to make friends with his friends, and allows Alan, who for many years had no family, say proudly to his friends, "My folks are coming."

People at Baptist Medical Center are being supportive and helpful. Dr. Carpenter (my boss) has made it possible for me to be granted a Family Medical Leave that allows me to come and go as needed and my job status will not change. I can think of no one else I would rather be working for at this time.

Fred says for the first time in his life he thinks he understands what it means to be comforted.

We knew going into this marriage we did not have fifty years and so we have lived it fully and well each day with a sense of gratitude that it was ours. So in that respect, we have not had to make any changes in the way we live with each other now. That is good.

It means there are no secrets, and no holding back to be strong for the other. We are simply present with one another. If we want to cry, that is fine, the other just holds on and often joins in the weeping.

If we are angry, that is okay too. The other validates that and gives encouragement and never thinks it is directed to them. If we need time alone, that is never misunderstood. We're always here and present when the other returns. We still laugh a lot and can find funny moments in this journey we are on.

Do we resent the cancer? You bet. The doctor told us he might live six months. We'd hoped for at least ten years together, maybe more. We've had three.

Do I get scared? Oh yes. The most peaceful years of my life I have known with Fred. What if I can't pull that off when he is not here?

Would we have not married if we'd known this is all we'd have? No. So in the midst of the incredible pain, we find we have much for which to give thanks.

He has been for me, above all, a safe place to feel my feelings. He has quietly accepted my pain, my fears, and my love, as though all were equally important. He looks at me and touches me with a tenderness I only thought was in romance novels.

He has made himself a friend of my friends, a part of my family, a support with my co-workers, a person I can count on. If I wanted to do something, he wanted to be part of it. What was important to me was important to him. Having been loved by this man means I am a richer person. How can I stay too long in resentment when all I feel is gratitude?

It is hard to talk about this in person because there is so much inside of me...and when I'm asked how we are doing, it comes out as "we're doing okay." Old habits are hard to break. But Fred says it best: "It's like finding a pile of dog shit in the mailbox. When you realize what it is, you have to work around it very carefully." It is—and we do.

Love,
Charlotte

Second Letter to Judy
Two weeks after Fred's death

Dear Judy:

When we married three years ago, we knew we were not going to celebrate a golden wedding anniversary and we determined then not to waste a minute of it. No stiff upper lips for us in any situation, and certainly not in the dying time.

It was a privilege for me to help him die and a great comfort to have you, my other co-workers and friends and family help both of us do it as we had wished—with grace and courage. I think we pulled it off. Thank you for being on our team.

I told my kids that I hope if they learned nothing else from mine and Fred's time together, that they learned there are very few things that are "big deals," that the greatest gifts of love are truth and kindness, touching and listening, and that love *always* means saying *I am sorry* when you hurt someone—and then working together to see what you must change so that it doesn't happen again.

Following are some writings I have entered in my journal, without recording who said them. I wish I knew so I could say thank you. But perhaps in your own times of grief, you may find them helpful, too, so I want to share.

• Growth comes in unexpected ways from the nooks and crannies of our life experiences. In death and grief we do not need as much protection from painful experiences as we need the boldness to face them. If we choose to love, then we must also have the courage to grieve.

• When faced with grief, it is important to take the time to integrate this or any loss in our lives so that even though someone is gone, our capacity to love is not gone also.

• The most beautiful people we will ever know are those who have known defeat, known suffering, known struggle, known loss, and have found their way out of the depths. These persons have an appreciation, sensitivity and an understanding of life that fills them with compassion, gentleness, and a deep loving concern. Beautiful people do not just happen.

If this person is right, then many of us are on our way to being gorgeous and wonderful!

My love and gratitude.
Charlotte

Third Letter to Judy
One month after Fred's death

Dear Judy:

I am going through a really hard time right now. I discover that I put off going to sleep at night. I read and read until I can hardly keep my eyes open.

The minute I turn out the light, the tears start. The pain looms incredibly big in front of me and often I turn the light back on and try to read some more or watch TV or do laundry or something—trying very hard to avoid the pain.

I suppose the numbness and total exhaustion of the past three months are wearing off and feelings are coming up easier. It seems that tears are not even adequate to express what I am feeling deep inside.

I sometimes wonder how people really do get through this. I realize I haven't even begun and at times that is absolutely overwhelming.

I love you very much and continue to be grateful you are in my life. I find great comfort in knowing you are there as I go through this year. I can't imagine the horror of feeling totally alone through a time of grief. I am not. And I am full of thanks for that.

My love,
Charlotte

Fourth Letter to Judy
Three months after Fred's death

Dear Judy:

The numbness that surrounded me at the beginning was a blessing and necessary to get me through the weeks that followed.

At about three months, I am told a time of depression is normal. I am being normal and I resent it.

The pain is like a big ache in my heart. It doesn't ever go away. The tears are close to the surface at all times. It is much harder work to be tough and hold it together. It is easier to be angry than to be sad. I have to be very aware of my anger so I won't hurt anyone with it, but it is usually the sadness that I don't want anyone to see.

Why is it so hard for me to let anyone see the pain, the grief? As a preacher's kid, I spent a lifetime pretending that everything was okay when it wasn't okay at all. I find I am trying to do that again.

As I write, the lump in my throat is growing and the tears are beginning to spill down my face. And I find I am struggling to keep the tears inside. I am beginning to understand my clients in a different way. I've now "been there."

I have changed nothing in our house since Fred died. All our pictures and memories surround me and I find that very comforting. The one room I have barely touched is our office area…his desk…my desk…I know I don't need both. Mine is nicer, his is bigger. Both are being used and all the pictures of me that were on his desk are still there. I can't put them away. It feels like if I change that room and his desk and his pictures, he will really be gone. I can't stand that…and the tears are running.

There are times I write in my journal, "I don't want to live without him." I don't think that means I want to die. But the thought circles slowly in my head. I promise if I think that is a serious thought, I will let you know.

Quite often I become aware that I am holding my breath and my entire body is almost rigid. My poor beat-up back from the fall of 1979 is reacting to that. My back feels "locked up." Lots of physical pain.

Most evenings I come home from work, undress and lie down. Sometimes I stay down all evening. I feel exhausted, yet I can't turn out the light. Since Fred and I married, we have gone to sleep spooned with each other. Now the aloneness hits me hardest when I turn out the light. I try to avoid that.

I am being told this is normal. Since when does normal look so great? I want to rise above it. I want to skip the grief work. Yet I know this is one I must do, one pain I must lean into. My love for/with/from Fred was too special to skip the grieving.

In many ways, he is the first person I ever allowed myself to really need.

He saw me in every way possible. He held me when the tears felt as though they would never stop...and now he isn't here. I think I am dying, too. I can't imagine how I can ever be okay again.

> With gratitude,
> Charlotte

Fifth Letter to Judy
12 months after Fred's death

Dear Judy:

What I have learned from Fred's death—so far.

That no matter how hard I try, there will always be "loose ends"...those things over which I have no control. For example, I wanted to be with Fred when he died, holding his hand, just being there—and it didn't happen that way. I was out of the house on an errand. So I must learn to live with the "loose ends" of my life.

In times of intense pain, it is easy to slip back into old coping patterns. For me that means, numbing the feelings, acting as if everything is all right, isolating, "shutting down." And the old messages are strong, "Try harder, do better, be perfect." But sometimes I need another person to see it and remind me that wherever I am today is all right.

Our time together was short, appreciated, not taken for granted. We were "up to date" when he died. Nothing had been left unsaid.

I am beginning to understand how important it is to quit focusing on what I don't have in my life and begin to look at what I do have...to not make my grief a "shrine," but to live the life I have with gratitude and not waste it in self pity.

At first, the missing him, the sadness, was so big it overwhelmed me. Now I have days when the gratitude is bigger than the sadness.

My prayer has moved from "Help me just get through the day" to "Give me the courage to dwell on what I have left, not what I have lost."

Thanks,
Charlotte

Sixth Letter to Judy
17 months after Fred's death

Dear Judy:

For a class assignment, my young twelve-year-old daughter once wrote: "Fall—when God makes even the dying time of the world beautiful."

This November, these words have come to me again.

After the death of Fred to cancer, I have felt as though I too was dying. It is the aloneness and the emptiness and the absence of his presence, his laughter, his warmth, his hugs and my "safe place."

How can I see this as a beautiful time—I who like answers and neat tidy packages and finished projects and everything in its place? The bills are paid, the insurance is collected, the trust is in place for his children and I am left waiting...something I've never been good at. I resent waiting. I find it inconvenient. Fred called it anticipation. I just called it a waste of time.

And what is it I am waiting for? Something to fill up the emptiness? Someone to take his place and make me feel alive again? People have taught me lessons on living, loving, communicating and relating, how to cook and sew, how to swim and play tennis, but no one ever taught me how to wait.

I realize I am judging myself harshly. I say to myself, "If you would just get a better attitude, then you wouldn't be depressed and discouraged." Do you know of anyone who teaches lessons on how to get a better attitude when someone you love has died? I pity the poor well-meaning person who may say that to me someday.

All I know is that in my despair and loneliness, I am often unaware of what is happening around me, because nothing else seems very important, compared to my pain.

And so I am left with the question, "How do I make this dying time of the world beautiful?" Perhaps all I can do is ask God to participate in my pain, to come in to it and be present with me, to bear it alongside me.

Thanks for always being there and knowing I can always talk to you about it.

Loving you.
Charlotte

Gifts in the Darkness

> I like living. I have sometimes been wildly, despairingly, acutely miserable and racked with sorrow, but through it all I still know quite certainly that just to be alive is a grand thing.
>
> —Agatha Christie

The accident at age forty brought a broken body. The divorce at age fifty meant a broken relationship. Now I was faced with a broken heart.

Even though I had taught classes on grief and helped to establish the Calm Waters support groups for grieving children, I did not have a clue how grief *felt*.

It is difficult and slow and wearing. I can also tell you I don't believe it ever ends, but I do believe it changes. I have gradually come to see that loss—whether of a limb or of a relationship or a death of someone you love—is a chapter in my life and as long as I am breathing, there will be more chapters to be lived.

At first the aloneness and the sadness was so big it overwhelmed me, but eventually I began to have days when the gratitude was bigger than the sadness.

A friend helped me understand it is okay to take breaks from your grief—going to work or taking a walk or seeing a movie or sharing a cup of coffee with a friend. The grief will always be there when you get back.

I gradually began to quit focusing on what I didn't have in my life and began to look—intentionally—at what I did have. When I speak of intentionally focusing on the good, I am reminded of my friend Beverly Reardon, a cancer survivor, who has kept ten years of gratitude journals, in which she has written each day a list of five things for which she is thankful. It doesn't mean she forgets the cancer, but it does mean she recognizes there are also great, good things in her life as well.

I guess it is all about finding a balance because I realized it didn't help to make my grief a shrine. That doesn't mean I thought the grief and loss were over and forgotten, but at some point, like Beverly, I chose to intentionally live the life I have with gratitude and not waste it in self-pity. Fred would want that.

During those first few months following Fred's death, I again looked back into the journals and was reminded of the many ways I'd been helped through the accident and the divorce, and I believed I'd be given what I needed to walk through this time. I saw the lessons I had learned and it helped keep me centered, at a time when I felt like I could easily break into hundreds of little pieces.

Other gifts also came to me from my past. One was a memory of my father, who had died five years earlier, and another was a written note from my daughter, Jayna.

The gift from my father was a line from one of his

sermons that began to pop into my mind. As a preacher's kid, I've heard thousands of sermons in my lifetime, and a few of them apparently remain in my head and in my heart.

When I would hit those days and nights when I did not think I could bear another day or take another step, I would hear him preaching.

One particular sermon was based on the Twenty-third Psalm. After he read the fourth verse, *"Even though I walk through the darkest valley, I fear no evil; for you are with me,"* my father went on to say that he believed the most important word in verse four was the word "through." He did not see the valley as a place you built a house and lived out your life. It was a temporary place—a space you passed through.

With the memory of his voice guiding me, I would take the next step, get out of bed, go to work, go to lunch with a friend, go to visit my grandchildren. I just *kept on keeping on*, as they say, hanging on to a thread of hope that there would come a day when I would walk again into the light.

The note from my daughter was tucked away in a box of old letters and dated Easter 1983, four years following my climbing accident. Jayna had been with me the day of my accident in 1979. When she wrote the note she was a twenty-year-old college student at Baylor University.

She had always been good at looking behind my brave facade and knowing when I was depressed and angry because of the ever-present pain and limitations. I also lived with some guilt because I knew I should have died and I should feel grateful, but instead all I wanted to do was complain. For some reason I never figured out that you could complain about the pain and find things for which to be grateful at the same time.

And that particular weekend was proving to be a difficult one.

On Easter Sunday morning, we were sitting in church and in the middle of the sermon Jayna leaned over and took an offering envelope from the back of the pew in front of us and began to write. When she finished, she passed the note to me and I read:

> Jesus—sure He died for the downtrodden and the weary, for the poor in pocketbook and in spirit, for the ugliness that this world brings, but He also died for the strong, who sometimes need to be not so tough and for the givers who sometimes need to receive. He also died for you, Mom. Being a strong person means handling the hurt, but it has never meant not feeling it.

The message on that note from thirteen years before came to me again in my time of grief, reminding me that it was okay for me to feel *not so tough*, to receive when I didn't have much to give, and that feeling my grief did not mean I wasn't being a strong person.

Again and again during those days when I felt I was living in a kind of black hole with absolutely no insight as to how I would function on the other side, I discovered my faith held me fast, anchored me, sustained me, and gave me hope when all I felt was despair.

The scripture verse that lived in my head and heart was Isaiah 40:31,

...but those who wait on the Lord will renew their strength. They will soar on wings like eagles; they will run and not grow weary, they will walk and not be faint.

I discovered a strength and courage within me that would not allow me to give up.

I discovered that I am a woman who simply refuses to wallow in self pity for very long, not because I am noble, but because I soon tire of it and find it boring.

I am also quick to tell you that anyone with a realistic view of life understands there is no "happily ever after," and therefore it is important to make the most of each day. I began to understand if I stay in the regret and the sorrow of *who* or *what* is no longer part of my life, then I will miss the *what* and the *who* that is in my present moment.

I eventually found a willingness to say goodbye to how it was, so that I could be free to embrace and say hello to the way things are now.

Over and over throughout this book, I write what I have learned—about life and about myself. I have come to believe that self-knowledge can be a valuable tool that will help us embrace who we are and understand what we want to celebrate and what we desire to change.

Speaking of change, I found my life wasn't over at all. New opportunities, new adventures and new friends were just ahead.

One of the most fun happenings came from my friend Patsy Hutchens. She came to me one day in my third year as a widow and said, "It is time for you to have a life." She took me by the hand and enrolled me in ballroom dancing lessons and at age fifty-nine, this Baptist preacher's kid finally learned to dance!

My instructor Nick Felix thought he was just teaching routine lessons, but what neither of us knew was that learning to dance would provide for me a road to healing. I've always thought, however, that my friend Patsy knew—and she was right.

When you are dancing to lovely music with an instructor or a partner who knows how to lead you, you become centered in the moment. It provides a brief respite from the pain that waits outside the door.

In the months that followed, fellow student Bill Horne, Jr., a young CPA from Ada, provided many evenings of dancing for the sheer fun of it. Bill became one of my closest friends and remains so to this day.

Through it all, I learned you couldn't dance and hold on to sadness. Dancing for me served as a reminder that life was not over, and that in the midst of the grief, it is important to allow times for joy and laughter.

I understand the psalmist who wrote in Psalms 30:11:

> You have turned my mourning into dancing;
> you have taken away my sackcloth (clothes of
> mourning) and clothed me with joy.

Courageous Risks Are Life Giving

Courageous risks are life giving, they help you grow, make you brave and better than you think you are.

—Joan L. Curcio

Dancing brought joy and play into my life. A position as director of the newly created James Hall Jr. Center for Mind, Body and Spirit brought challenge and new work that I find very satisfying and that I believe in and enjoy.

Our aim is to help individuals understand they are an important part of their own health care team, working together with their physicians. Whether it is facing a health crisis or desiring to lead a healthy lifestyle, we work to heighten their self-awareness and teach tools that will be useful.

In 1999 *The Oklahoman* invited me to write a weekly column. And oh, the marvelous people I have met because of it.

They write letters that come in the mailbox, send emails that show up on my computer screen and a few have stopped by my office to say hello in person.

Others telephone and invite me to speak to their churches, their civic groups, their businesses—and a few have even asked if they could use one of the columns in their newsletter or their church worship service or as a handout to their staff. I am always amazed and delighted.

However, in the midst of the good things that were happening and the knowledge that I was going to survive once more, there was always increasing back pain. In 2001, the back pain reached an all time high.

This time it could not be ignored and it could not be managed. Vertebrae had slipped and were pressing down on the nerves in my lower back and eventually I was having difficulty walking. This time it was my friends Tony and Claire Puckett who walked most closely beside me and gave me a safe place to lean.

Through the skillful hands of orthopedic surgeon, Dr. James Odor, I underwent a successful back surgery and for the first time in twenty-two years I was out of the daily, grinding wearing pain. It felt as though I'd been given a new life.

When Dr. Odor asked me later, "Do you wish we'd done it sooner?" my answer was, "Of course!" And yet I also know that living with unending pain for all those years has made me a better friend, a better therapist and a more compassionate person.

Dr. Rachel Naomi Remen in her book, *My Grandfather's Blessings*, writes:

How tempting it is to put the struggle behind

us as quickly as possible and get on with our lives. Life might be easier then but far less genuine. Perhaps the wisdom lies in engaging the life you have been given as fully and courageous as possible and not letting go until you find the unknown blessing that is in everything.

Today, without the constant pain and having a work I love, old and new friendships I treasure, warm and loving friendships with my four adult children and eight grandchildren, I have to tell you that I still miss Fred. I always will.

But now I know that when you love and are loved by someone as special as he, they never leave you. They are always a part of you and live forever in your head and in your heart. I think he would be pleased with how I have lived in the years since his passing.

And now back to where I began this book. *I don't know of anyone who lives a long time that has not been wounded in some way. It is called life, and it happens to us all.*

I do not think my story is any more spectacular than yours. But it is my story. And many of you have asked me to share it.

By being willing to tell my story, I have discovered it often builds a bridge to someone else moving through a dark time. It provides a connection to others who might otherwise think I could never understand how they feel.

But I am still left with the question, "How do I—and you—make this dying time of the world beautiful?" Perhaps by being willing to tell our own stories, because we all have one; to share our life experiences through the dark and difficult times, so they can become useful and not wasted; to remember there are lessons to be learned and gifts to be found that will help us keep our balance.

The glass is sometimes half full…sometimes half empty. It's called life. And the one thing I believe is that there is no need to make this journey through life alone.

My friend Mike Bumgarner reminded me of this in a note he wrote to me following Fred's death.

> As you make this journey through grief, I am one of those people standing by the side of the road with my hand held out. Any time you need to lean a little, just grab hold.

As I have finished writing this part of my story about Fred's death and my grief, I searched for the words to tell you where I am now. And then Marti McClure of Oklahoma City sent me a quote by writer Anne Lamott who says it well:

> As you grow older, you will lose someone you can't live without and your heart will be badly broken, and the bad news is that you never completely get over the loss of a beloved person. But this is also the good news. They live forever in your broken heart that doesn't heal back up. And you come through. It's like having a broken leg that never heals perfectly, that still hurts when the weather is cold, but you learn to dance with the limp.

I am choosing to dance—limp and all. I invite you to join me.

Life Is a Continuum

Your world is as big as you make it,
I know, for I used to abide
In the narrowest nest in a corner,
My wings pressing close to my side.
I battered the cordons around me
And cradled my wings on the breeze,
Then soared to the uttermost reaches
With rapture, with power, with ease!
————Georgia Douglas Johnson

I have discovered there are always things that frighten us as we go along on this journey through life. I believe the wise person gets to know their fears well. Little is gained by resisting them.

When I can simply acknowledge that which scares me, I find I can stop struggling and relax—it is a simple acceptance. After all, the fear is usually there for a reason. For me, it has been a fear of heights that goes back to my fortieth year. I didn't know the extent of that fear until two years following the accident.

J. T. and I were in San Francisco and we got into a glass elevator on the outside of a building. As the elevator rose and the ground receded I experienced an adrenaline rush of intense fear—not anxiety—but terror and panic. Later I would recognize it as a Post Traumatic Stress reaction. My body had remembered the fall in the Forty Foot Hole Canyon.

From that point on, I simply avoided any kind of exposure that would bring on that feeling. After all, one can live without riding Ferris wheels or climbing cliffs.

Then, twenty-six years later, at a charity auction in 2005, businessman Jim Daniel bought a ride in a 1945 Stearman—a bi-plane with two seats and open cockpit. It's the kind of plane that Navy pilots flew in World War II.

Jim is a friend of the pilot and owner of the plane, Paul Odom, II. Because he'd already flown with Paul, Jim offered the flight to me.

While there was a part of me that thought it sounded like a grand and exciting adventure, there was another part of me that was frightened. Just thinking of it brought panic, my breath became shallow and fear welled up inside me.

As a marriage and family therapist, I work with people all the time who are afraid of something from their own life experiences. Fear of trusting, fear of being hurt again, fear of stepping out into a new adventure, fear of making changes. And it is not uncommon at some point in therapy to encourage them to face the fear.

Easier said than done, I now realize.

Faced with the opportunity to face my fear, what was I going to do? I could simply say, "No, thank you, I pass." But I found myself not wanting to do that. I wanted the adventure, the experience. I wanted to tell my grandchildren that we are never too old to face any fear. I wanted to honor the men and women who sit in my office and who are willing to face theirs.

At age sixty-seven, no one would have thought badly

of me for not doing it. No one would have been surprised if I had declined. But I knew I was not doing this for anyone else, only myself.

I prepared for the flight for more than a year. I placed a big picture of the plane in my office. I imagined the ride. Just imagining it would bring on the panic. I practiced deep, diaphragmatic, relaxing breathing. I worked on desensitization by going with hospital security guards out on the rooftop of Baptist Medical Center—eleven floors up. I took seriously the advice of pilot Paul Odom—look up and out, not down.

Then in the spring of 2006, I returned to the Forty Foot Hole Canyon. It had been twenty-seven years since I was last there.

The place where I had fallen felt eerily familiar. It was still beautiful, quiet and peaceful—a narrow canyon with a swimming hole at one end.

I was surprised that I did not feel the intense panic. Apparently the practicing of deep breathing and pilot Odom's advice to look up and out, not down, was working.

Another interesting observance that day was that instead of focusing on the accident, the brokenness and the pain of all those years, I found myself remembering the adventure, the sense of accomplishment and the surge of adrenalin that would hit me when I would finally touch bottom and my first thought being, "I want to do it again!"

As I stood looking at the sheer drop of 125 feet, I wondered how I had survived. It is the same sense of awe we have when we look back on the painful and broken times in our lives and wonder how we are still standing.

In July 2006 I donned a leather helmet and goggles

and climbed into the front seat of that bi-plane. I trusted the pilot. I trusted myself to manage the fear when it started rising.

As the plane rolled down the runway I looked up and out and took very deep breaths. Then the plane lifted into the air—and I flew.

The day was shared with my thirteen-year-old granddaughter Jessica, who had her own turn at flying with Mr. Odom, and Steve Sisney, photographer for *The Oklahoman* who was there to take pictures. Steve was the right one for that job because he later told me he is a friend of "...timid felines and fraidy-cats of all kinds." And I was a "fraidy-cat" that day for sure.

Don't misunderstand, the fear is not gone, but it has been faced and I have confidence that when it comes again, I will be able to face it. I also believe it will help me to be more patient and gentle and respectful of people who come to me for help in facing their own fears.

I want to remember when the changes of life come, friends will be there to walk beside me, gifts will be found even in the darkest times, important lessons will be learned and verses of scripture I memorized as a child will resonate in my head and heart—verses like Matthew 28:20 where Jesus says, "...surely I am with you always." I look back and see I counted on that.

Where do I go from here? I do not know, but I am no longer afraid of the future.